Colorful Blessings

Psalms of Peace and Hope

A COLORING BOOK OF FAITHFUL EXPRESSION

In GOD I have put my trust

psalm 56:11

ILLUSTRATIONS BY DEBORAH MULLER

ST. MARTIN'S GRIFFIN

NEW YORK

This is the day which the Lord hath made; we will rejoice and be glad in it.

Psalm 118:24

From the end of the earth will
I cry unto thee, when my heart
is overwhelmed: lead me to the
rock that is higher than I.

Psalm 61:2

Praise ye the Lord. O give thanks unto the Lord; for he is good: for his mercy endureth for ever.

Psalm 106:1

Why art thou cast down, O my soul?
and why art thou disquieted in me?
hope thou in God: for I shall yet praise
him for the help of his countenance.

Psalm 42:5

Psalm 122:8

Peace be within me.

The Lord shall preserve thy going
out and thy coming in from this
time forth, and even for evermore.

Psalm 121:8

As the hart panteth after the water brooks, so panteth my soul after thee, O God.

Psalm 42:1

This is my comfort in my affliction:
for thy word hath quickened me.

Psalm 119:50

I WAITED PATIENTLY FOR THE LORD; AND HE INCLINED UNTO ME, AND HEARD MY CRY.

PSALM 40:1

Let, I pray thee, thy merciful
kindness be for my comfort,
according to thy word unto
thy servant.

Psalm 119:76

The Lord will bless his people with peace

Psalm 29:11b

Lead me in thy truth, and teach me:
for thou art the God of my salvation;
on thee do I wait all the day.

Psalm 25:5

Peace and Hope

Psalm 107:8

He loveth righteousness and
judgment: the earth is full of
the goodness of the Lord.

Psalm 33:5

I will call upon the Lord, who is
worthy to be praised: so shall I be
saved from mine enemies.

Psalm 18:3

But I will hope
continually, and will
yet praise thee
more and more.

Psalm 71:14

Keep me as the apple of the eye, hide
me under the shadow of thy wings.

Psalm 17:8

Seek Peace

Psalm 34:14

But thou, O LORD, are a shield for me, my glory, and the lifter up of mine head.

Psalm 3:3

HE ONLY IS MY ROCK AND MY SALVATION: HE IS MY DEFENCE; I SHALL NOT BE GREATLY MOVED.

PSALM 62:2

I love the LORD, because he
hath heard my voice and
my supplications.

Psalm 116:1

The LORD also will be a refuge
for the oppressed, a refuge in
times of trouble.

Psalm 4:8

Be glad in the LORD, and rejoice,
ye righteous: and shout for joy,
all ye that are upright in heart.

Psalm 32:11

Let the words of my mouth, and
the meditation of my heart, be
acceptable in thy sight, O Lord,
my strength, and my redeemer.

Psalm 19:14

I will love thee, O Lord, my strength.

Psalm 18:1

It is God that girdeth me with strength,
and maketh my way perfect.

Psalm 18:32

But let all those that put their trust in thee rejoice: let them ever shout for joy

PSALM 5:11

Remember, O LORD, thy tender
mercies and thy lovingkindness;
for they have been ever of old.

Psalm 25:6

He shall receive the blessing
from the LORD, and righteousness
from the God of his salvation.

Psalm 24:5

O keep my soul, and deliver me:
let me not be ashamed; for I put
my trust in thee.

Psalm 25:20

Be of good courage, and he shall Strengthen Your heart.

Psalm 31:24

Our help is in the name of the
LORD, who made heaven and earth.

Psalm 124:8

One thing have I desired of the LORD,
that will I seek after; that I may dwell in
the house of the LORD all the days of my
life, to behold the beauty of the LORD,
and to inquire in his temple.

Psalm 27:4

I will sing unto the LORD, because
he hath dealt bountifully with me.

Psalm 13:6

In thee, O Lᴏʀᴅ, do I put my trust:
let me never be put to confusion.

Psalm 71:1

Cast thy burden upon the Lord, and he shall sustain thee

Psalm 55:22

Preserve me, O God: for in
thee do I put my trust.

Psalm 16:1

Wait on the Lord: be of good courage, and he shall strengthen thine heart

Psalm 27:14

The troubles of my heart are
enlarged: O bring thou me out
of my distresses.

Psalm 25:17

Even there shall thy hand lead me, and thy right hand shall hold me.

Psalm 139:10

Therefore my heart is glad, and
my glory rejoiceth: my flesh also
shall rest in hope.

Psalm 16:9

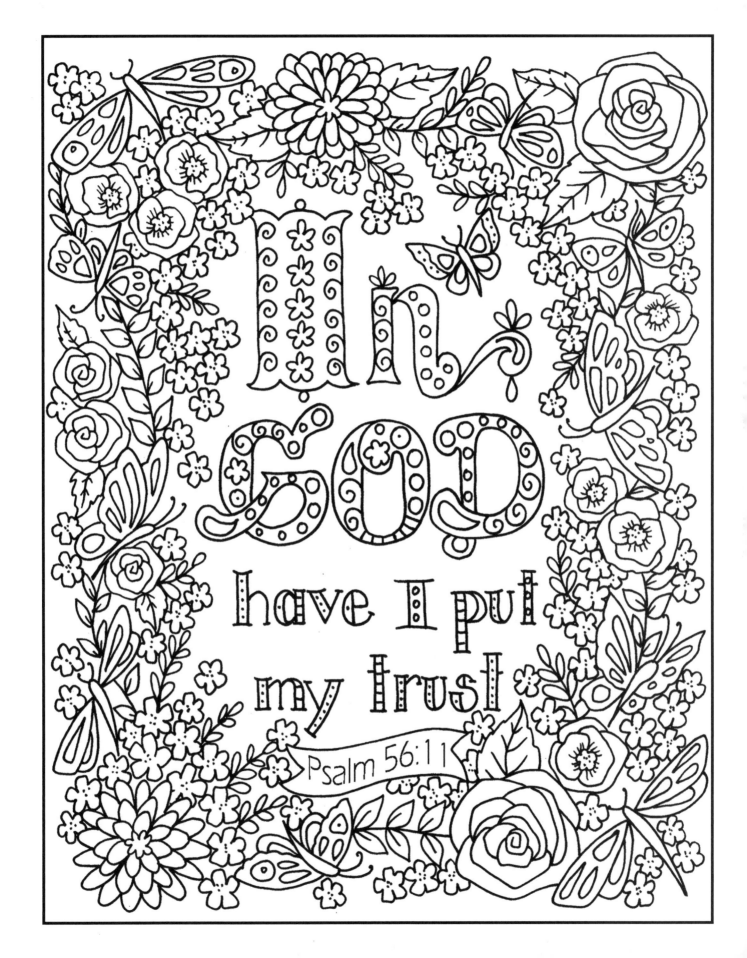

In GOD have I put my trust

Psalm 56:11

Let integrity and uprightness
preserve me; for I wait on thee.

Psalm 25:21

They that sow in tears shall reap in joy.

Psalm 126:5

I have called upon thee, for thou
wilt hear me, O God: incline thine
ear unto me, and hear my speech.

Psalm 17:6

Pray for the peace of Jerusalem:
they shall prosper that love thee.

Psalm 122:6

The Lord is my STRENGTH and my SHIELD; my heart trusted in him

PSALM 28:7

Hear, O Lord, when I cry with my
voice: have mercy also upon me,
and answer me.

Psalm 27:7

For thou art my hope, O Lord GOD:
thou art my trust from my youth.

Psalm 71:5

Unto thee, O Lᴏʀᴅ, do I lift
up my soul.

Psalm 25:1

Thou art God
Psalm 90:2

O continue thy lovingkindness
unto them that know thee; and thy
righteousness to the upright in heart.

Psalm 36:10

I will sing of the mercies of the Lord Forever with my mouth will I make known thy faithfullness to all generations

Psalm 89:1

The LORD is my light and my salvation;
whom shall I fear? the LORD is the strength
of my life; of whom shall I be afraid?

Psalm 27:1

Because he hath inclined his
ear unto me, therefore will I call
upon him as long as I live.

Psalm 116:2

Remember the word unto thy
servant, upon which thou has
caused me to hope.

Psalm 119:49

For the LORD is good; his mercy
is everlasting; and his truth
endureth to all generations.

Psalm 100:5

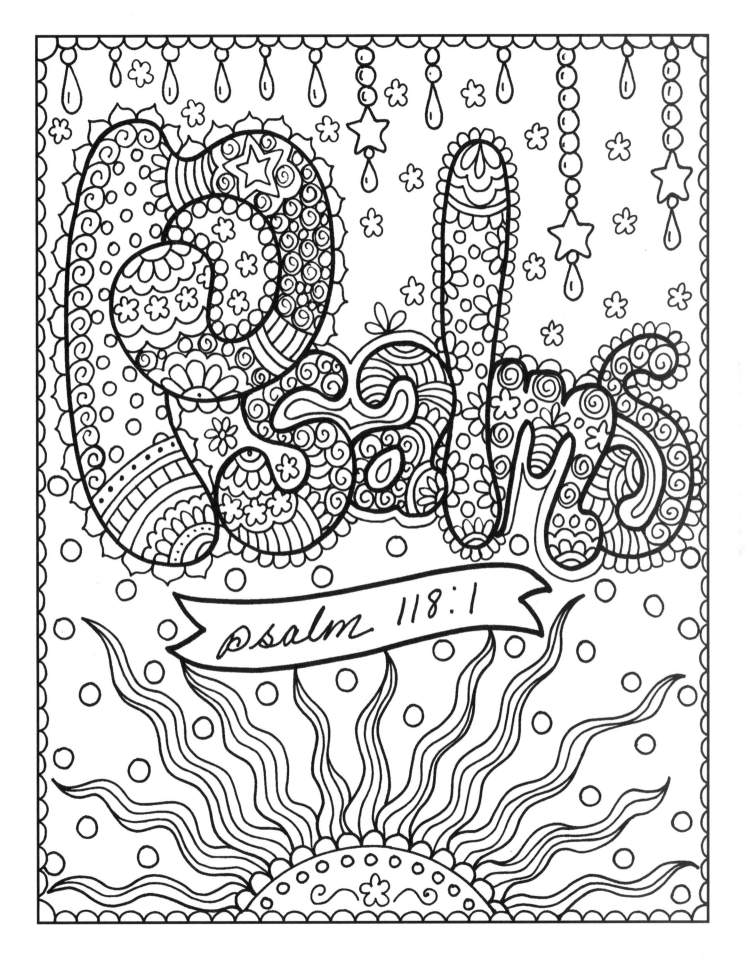

So teach us to number our days,
that we may apply our hearts
unto wisdom.

Psalm 90:12

psalm 56:3

What time
I am afraid,
I will
trust in thee.

But it is good for me to draw
near to God: I have put my trust
in the Lord God, that I may
declare all thy works.

Psalm 73:28

Psalm 145:18

Let all those that seek thee rejoice
and be glad in thee: let such as
love thy salvation say continually,
The Lord be magnified.

Psalm 40:16

For thou, Lord, art good, and ready to forgive Psalm 86:5

I sought the LORD, and he heard me,
and delivered me from all my fears.

Psalm 34:4

Thou hast turned for me my
mourning into dancing: thou
hast put off my sackcloth, and
girded me with gladness.

Psalm 30:11

For thou art my rock and my
fortress; therefore for thy name's
sake lead me, and guide me.

Psalm 31:3

I will speak of the glorious
honour of thy majesty, and
of thy wondrous works.

Psalm 145:5

But I have trusted in thy mercy;

my heart shall rejoice in thy salvation.

Psalm 13:5

My heart is fixed, O God, my heart
is fixed: I will sing and give praise.

Psalm 57:7

Thou wilt shew me the path of life: in thy presence is fulness of joy; at thy right hand there are pleasures for evermore.

Psalm 16:11

I will be glad and rejoice in thy mercy:
for thou hast considered my trouble;
thou hast known my soul in adversities.

Psalm 31:7

The Lord is my rock, and my fortress, and my deliverer; my God, my strength, in whom I will trust; my buckler, and the horn of my salvation, and my high tower.

Psalm 18:2

They that trust in the Lᴏʀᴅ shall be as mount Zion, which cannot be removed, but abideth for ever.

Psalm 125:1

Though I walk in the midst of
trouble, thou wilt revive me: thou
shalt stretch forth thine hand
against the wrath of mine enemies,
and thy right hand shall save me.

Psalm 138:7

I have set the LORD always before
me; because he is at my right hand,
I shall not be moved.

Psalm 16:8

my cup runneth over

Psalm 23:5

Peace be within thy walls, and
prosperity within thy palaces.

Psalm 122:7

THE EARTH IS THE LORD'S, AND THE FULNESS THEREOF; THE WORLD, AND THEY THAT DWELL THEREIN.

PSALM 24:1

God is our refuge and strength,
a very present help in trouble.

Psalm 46:1

Blessed are the
undefiled in the way,
who walk in the
law of the Lord.

Psalm 119:1

For our heart shall rejoice in
him, because we have trusted
in his holy name.

Psalm 33:21

And now, Lord, what wait I for? my hope is in thee. Psalm 39:7

Create in me a clean heart, O God;
and renew a right spirit within me.

Psalm 51:10

Bless the LORD, O my soul,
and forget not all his benefits.

Psalm 103:2

My soul fainteth for thy salvation:
but I hope in thy word.

Psalm 119:81

In his days shall the righteous flourish; and abundance of peace so long as the moon endureth.   Psalm 72:7

I will lift up mine eyes unto the hills,
from whence cometh my help.

Psalm 121:1

Who forgiveth all thine iniquities; who healeth all thy diseases

Psalm 103:3

The righteous cry, and the LORD
heareth, and delivereth them out
of all their troubles.

Psalm 34:17

The Lord is merciful and gracious, slow to anger, and plenteous in mercy.

Psalm 103:8

The LORD is good to all: and his tender
mercies are over all his works.

Psalm 145:9

Sing unto him, sing   psalms

unto him; talk ye of all his

wondrous works.

Psalm 105:2

The Lord is thy keeper: the Lord is thy shade upon thy right hand. The sun shall not smite thee by day, nor the moon by night.

Psalm 121:5–6

The LORD is nigh unto them that
are of a broken heart; and saveth
such as be of a contrite spirit.

Psalm 34:18

Praise ye the Lord. I will praise the Lord with my whole heart, in the assembly of the upright, and in the congregation.

Psalm 111:1

Let my supplication come before thee:
deliver me according to thy word.

Psalm 119:170

THOU ART MY HIDING PLACE AND MY SHIELD: I HOPE IN THY WORD.

PSALM 119:114

Great peace have they which love thy
law: and nothing shall offend them.

Psalm 119:165